DARWIN'S ARK

DARWIN'S

POEMS BY
Philip Appleman

ILLUSTRATIONS BY
Rudy Pozzatti

ARK

Indiana University Press • Bloomington

Library of Congress Cataloging in Publication Data

Appleman, Philip, 1926–
  Darwin's ark.

  1. Darwin, Charles, 1809–1882—Poetry. 2. Natural
history—Poetry. 3. Evolution—Poetry. 4. Animals—
Poetry. I. Pozzatti, Rudy, 1925–   . II. Title.
PS3551.P6D3 1984   811'.54   83–49412
ISBN 0–253–11594–9

1 2 3 4 5 88 87 86 85 84

for MARGIE

"Morning is out there again . . ."

Contemplate a tangled bank,
clothed with many plants of many kinds,
with birds singing on the bushes,
with various insects flitting about,
and
with worms crawling through the damp earth:
these elaborately constructed forms
have all been produced by laws
acting around us.
Thus, from the war of nature,
from famine and death,
the production of the higher animals
directly follows.
There is grandeur in this view of life:
whilst this planet has gone
cycling on according to
the fixed law of gravity,
from so simple a beginning
endless forms most beautiful and
most wonderful have been
and are being
evolved.

CHARLES DARWIN

If the labours of men of science should ever
create any material revolution, direct or indi-
rect, in our condition, and in the impressions
which we habitually receive, the poet will
sleep then no more than at present; he will be
ready to follow the steps of the men of science,
. . . carrying sensations into the midst of the
objects of science itself. The remotest discov-
eries of the chemist, the botanist, or mineral-
ogist, will be as proper objects of the poet's art
as any upon which it can be employed . . .

WILLIAM WORDSWORTH

Contents

ACKNOWLEDGMENTS

Grateful acknowledgment is made to the editors of the following publications, in which some of the poems in this book first appeared.

Aloe: "Black-Footed Ferret Endangered"

Bluefish: "The Hand-Ax"

College English: "On the *Beagle*," "After the Faith-Healings"

Confrontation: "Gaminophobia," "Locophobia," "Bacardophobia"

Creel: "So Full of a Number of Things"

Indiana Review: "Staying Awake with Darwin"

Kentucky Poetry Review: "How Evolution Came to Indiana," "The Descent of Man," "In Andalucia," "State of Nature, 2 and 3," "Sexual Selection"

The Literary Review: "Reading Our Times"

Midwest Quarterly: "Darwin on Fourteenth Street"

The Nation: "How My Light Is Spent"

New York Times: "The Skeletons of Dreams"

North American Review: "Darwin's Bestiary"

Partisan Review: "Shamanophobia," "Mortiphobia"

Poetry: "State of Nature 1," "Mr. Extinction, Meet Ms. Survival," "Nostalgie de la Boue," "The Voyage Home"

Prairie Schooner: "Sea Otter Survival Assured"

Tendril: "Waldorf-Astoria Euphoria," "Peoria Euphoria," "Hunkydoria Euphoria"

"Sea Otter Survival Assured" was previously reprinted in *Summer Love and Surf* (Nashville: Vanderbilt University Press, 1968); "On the *Beagle*" was reprinted in *Open Doorways* (New York: W. W. Norton & Co., 1976).

PREFACE

I think that a man who wants to write in the twentieth century makes a great mistake if he doesn't begin by reading *The Origin of Species*. . . .

BASIL BUNTING

I consider myself lucky, as a poet, to have been interested in Charles Darwin all my adult life; but that had nothing to do with my schooling. As it turned out, it was (in a Shandean way) relevant to my experience of Darwin that I was conceived in the same month that John Thomas Scopes was arrested and indicted by a grand jury for the crime of teaching evolution to the schoolchildren of Dayton, Tennessee, and that in due course I was born in the same month that the legislature of the state of Mississippi duplicated the Tennessee anti-evolution law. My memory of those events is imperfect, but I conjure up the temper of the times from the historical fact that in the year of my birth, the famous evangelist Aimee Semple McPherson, concocting an alibi for an extended rendezvous with her lover, claimed to have been kidnapped by gamblers, dope peddlers, and evolutionists; and from the establishment, a year after my birth, of the American Anti-Evolution Association, an organization open to all citizens *except* "Negroes, Atheists, Infidels, Agnostics, Evolutionists, and habitual drunkards."

So by the time I started school, it was not surprising that the anti-evolutionary laws had spread to Arkansas and Florida, that there had been agitation for similar laws all around the country, and that high school and college teachers had been fired for mentioning evolution in the classroom. By the time I learned to read, textbook publishers had already got the message. The word "evolution" and the name of Darwin had been deleted from virtually all public-school textbooks, and continued to be banned, partly by law and partly by self-censorship, for four decades. The public schools of my Hoosier home town were no different from most others in America: in twelve years of education, including a high school course in biology, I never heard the name of Charles Robert Darwin. Across the nation, the invisible government of church fathers and school boards had in effect abolished a natural law from the schools.

It was, in retrospect, a rather astonishing feat, the educational equivalent of, say, the Flat Earth Society abolishing gravitation. So my fifty-eight classmates and I, like many thousands of our contemporaries around the country, graduated from high school totally ignorant of one of the most basic facts of life: the perpetual functioning of organic evolution.

(It would be gratifying if all that were now changed, but alas, recent studies indicate that even today, evolution is ignored in many American high school biology courses.)

Almost by accident, I finally did get around to reading *The Origin of Species*, which I had packed in my sea bag for a long trip in the Merchant Marine. I was the same age then as Darwin was when he set out on the *Beagle*, and because of his book, my trip, too, was a voyage of discovery. In 1948, before the paperback revolution, the only cheap and easily available editions of the classics of literature, science, and philosophy were the Everyman and Modern Library editions. Fortunately, there was a Modern Library "Giant" with *The Origin of Species* and *The Descent of Man* in one volume: exactly one thousand pages of small print. I still have the book, a bit dog-eared from thirty-five years of travel and use, and much underscored with the smudgy blue first-generation ball-point pens I carried to sea.

I read that book in noisy mess rooms, surrounded by cribbage-playing seamen. I read it in my bunk at night, the persistent bedlamp sometimes infuriating my watchmates. I read it on deck in the sunny waters of the Mediterranean, meanwhile collecting extra hazard pay because stray floating mines from World War II were still sinking ships there. The 1948 marginalia reinforce my memory of being interested in the mechanisms of natural selection, but the more detailed marginalia indicate that what most held my attention, in both *The Origin* and *The Descent*, was the information bearing upon the relation of human beings to the rest of nature, and the philosophical implications of evolution.

I am sure it is difficult for anyone reared in a more enlightened time and place to imagine the sense of exhilaration in a young person schooled in Midwestern fundamentalism, reading Darwin and understanding evolution for the very first time. But I recall that experience vividly: the overwhelming sanity that emerged from Darwin's clearly thought out and clearly written propositions; the relief at being finally released from a constrained allegiance to the incredible creation myths of Genesis; the profound satisfaction in knowing that one is truly and altogether a part of nature.

I couldn't have foreseen it at the time, but I have been reading Darwin ever since—*The Voyage of the Beagle, The Expression of the Emotions in*

Man and Animals, the books on barnacles, on earthworms, and on orchids, the journals, the notebooks, the autobiography—that whole prodigious Victorian labor of love. And I have also been writing about Darwin ever since: a doctoral dissertation, an abridged edition of *The Origin*, articles, lectures, chapters, reviews, the Norton Critical Edition, *Darwin*, and many poems.

Darwin was inspired with the idea of natural selection by reading Malthus; I was led to Malthus by reading Darwin, and became so concerned with overpopulation as to write a book about it, called *The Silent Explosion*, and to edit the Norton Critical Edition on Malthus. Many of the poems in this volume have their conceptual and emotional roots in the deplorably neglected problem of overpopulation. The continued proliferation of human bodies and human needs, with the resulting competition for limited resources, destruction of natural habitats, growing pollution of the environment, endangering of other species, even the threat of extinction itself: all of these are ultimately Malthusian as well as Darwinian themes, and they stir beneath the surface of many of these poems.

That accounts for the genesis of the poetry in this book, but not for the beautiful art work. My friend and colleague Rudy Pozzatti and I had talked for some years about working together on a book of Darwin poems with accompanying illustrations, especially of animals. Darwin's books are of course full of animals, so my poems are populated with them, too. I had always admired Rudy's handsome beasts in the *Bestiary of Bishop Theobaldus* (Indiana University Press, 1964), so a collaboration on the Darwin poems was appealing to me.

Over the past year it has been a pleasure to watch Rudy's drawings grow and develop and find their way into this book. Sharon Sklar has designed the elegant format. For many helpful suggestions, I am indebted first of all to my wife, Margie, as well as to my colleagues Roger Mitchell, Maura Stanton, Willis Barnstone, Donald Gray, and Kenneth Johnston. As this book is going into proofs, the Echo Press, a fine arts press in Bloomington, is also preparing an *édition de luxe* of eleven of these poems, with original lithographs by Rudy. Contemplating this tangled bank of varied activity, I feel privileged to thank all of these talented and generous friends.

P.A.
Bloomington, Indiana
April 1984

DARWIN'S ARK

I

Giants in the Earth

The world, it has often been remarked,
appears as if it had long
been preparing for the advent of man;
and this, in one sense, is strictly true,
for he owes his birth to a long line
of progenitors.
If any single link in this chain
had never existed,
man would not have been
exactly what he now is.
Unless we wilfully close our eyes,
we may, with our present knowledge,
approximately recognise our parentage,
nor need we feel ashamed of it.

CHARLES DARWIN

I suggest it is a true image of both scientists
and writers to see them all as a scattered pro-
cession of explorers, small as ants as compared
to the world, each climbing his grassblade to
view the universe, uttering triumphant cries
now called a poem, now a scientific fact, one
here, one there, until the world we know gets
mapped and remapped, over and over; that is
to say, gets invented again and again in every
generation . . .

SEAN O'FAOLAIN

The Skeletons of Dreams

He found giants
in the earth: Mastodon,
Mylodon, thigh bones
like tree trunks, Megatherium, skulls
big as boulders—once,
in this savage country, treetops
trembled at their passing.
But their passing was silent as snails,
silent as rabbits: nothing at all recorded
the day when the last of them came
crashing through creepers and ferns,
shaking the earth a final time,
leaving behind them crickets,
monkeys, and mice.
For think: at last it is nothing
to be a giant—the dream
of an ending haunts tortoise and Toxodon,
troubles the sleep of the woodchuck
and the bear.

Back home in his English garden,
Darwin paused in his pacing,
writing it down in italics
in the book at the back of his mind:
   When a species has vanished
   from the face of the earth,
   the same form never reappears . . .
So after our millions of years
of inventing a thumb and a cortex,
and after the long pain
of writing our clumsy epic,

we know we are mortal as mammoths,
we know the last lines of our poem.
And somewhere in curving space
beyond our constellations,
nebulae burn in their universal law:
nothing out there ever knew
that on one sky-blue planet
we dreamed that terrible dream.
Blazing along through black nothing
to nowhere at all, Mastodons of heaven,
the stars do not need our small ruin.

Nostalgie de la Boue

1

Out there in the cornfields, we knew
about mud, its personalities
as shifty as the snow
Eskimos have a dozen names for—
the muck in onionland, sponge
rubber of pastures, clay
that mooshed into guck to yank
your boots off—so full
of dormant seeds you could smell
in every squish of it
the brooding life: that
was mud you could call mud, not
this sissy sterile city stuff
in gutters and vacant lots;
in the little town I lived in, mud
was everywhere in April, when the snow
has taken final leave, but the grass
doesn't believe it, and big bare
patches in the lawn that in August were
triumphant crabgrass
are swamps of maple twigs, bark, debris
of winter, waiting to be earth,
and the hairless denizens of this land,
suspicious of heaven, wear
their sheepskins tight, knowing
that any minute the sky could fall,
shattering spring—and yet
they smell it, too, the promises:
perfume of mud in April,
all around us,
waiting.

2

We go back a long time together,
Hoosiers and mud: to devil summers

6

on Noble County farms, and weariness
no city work ever shared
with a back, the ache in our marrow dissolving
to memories of mosses, ferns,
protozoans in the soup
of ancestral mud: all
in our bones, out there in that little town
that looks like a game of tic-tac-toe
run wild, right-angle streets,
proud of their civilization, superimposed
on the Indiana Territory, contours
trod upon by deerskin moccasins
come on the lost land-bridges:
brittle streets laid over first
with gravel, then with bricks,
concrete, asphalt—generations
of style, paving over the mud;
there, in that formal
web, in April, forsythia
surprised the mud with prophecy
of dandelions, firecrackers,
hopscotch shade of maple trees, croquet balls
lumping along a rough back yard
toward the tragedy of
chrysanthemums.

3

They say build your houses on rock,
but in Noble County we built
on mud, and in April
a boy could stand on a white front porch,
lacy with spindles and railings,
and stare at the mud
and think about summer and a girl
in a window a mile away,
looking out at the mud, thinking
about a boy on a white front porch,
and a mile of wet earth

between them, as full of life
as the mud that bore flatworms and slugs,
the first amphibians, pioneers,
lizards and lemurs, and finally
upright silhouettes loping across
the mothering mud—on quiet nights,
as arrowheads bloomed in the dark of the moon,
we felt it all, and you
can feel it, too, closing your eyes,
holding your wrist, feeling the jellyfish
tugging the pulses: *there*
and *there*.

4

It was our birthright in Noble County, that
ancient ground, the farmers always
cursing the mud
but coaxing the tractors through it
somehow, spring plowing turning up
ten thousand years of spearheads—then
the Saturday trips to town, to buy
clodhopper shoes at Penney's
and popcorn at the old red wagon, and sit
in Chevvies parked at the curb,
loose jaws munching the salty corn,
watching the *Homo sapiens* strolling Main Street,
clutching their mates by the forearm, guarding
their young at their sides, waiting
for sun, and Sunday School, and the tail-
less primate with opposable thumbs
gripping his black book, baying
at sin, as April sun pours
purple through scenes of Creation, slanting
on pews of leathery muzzles and snouts;
and the fields of Indiana mud
go on unplowed, tractors waiting
for godless Monday, spring-
tooth harrows suspended in time,

and lawns that would soon be grass
for badminton, still mud,
and flagpoles all over town
rooted in mud, flowering stars
and stripes forever, and
on one white porch,
an accident of molecules
and history, looking like
a young boy standing in Sunday spring,
expectantly, as if
he could walk a mile
through mud, and speak to the girl
in the window—as if he could
step off that white porch into feelings
he will never have; but the house,
built on mud, will nevertheless
survive the boy and the girl; and this one
silent moment,
promising grass and the cool shade
of maples, is still out there
on a front porch
waiting.

State of Nature

1

This is how it's done: the queen
of beasts, prima donna, hunching
in dry grass, is perfectly
dry-grass, her contours
miming the landscape. Some
suns ago there had been
the zebra, before that the eland;
memories of feasting stir
through her veins, the call in the belly
like drumming hooves of antelope.
Muzzles nudging the soft shoots:
the old drama
begins again; her yellow eyes squint
like a kitten petted; her nose
twitches in the downwind tang—
the sudden bound: gazelles
stampede across the veldt, Keystone
Kops zig-
zagging in speeded-up film, until
the herd
strings
out,
tropical crack-the-whip, the weakest
tiring, fear in the breath,
death in the watery legs.
One pair of antlers falls
behind; now
the cat knows the shape of her dinner:
the beautiful Pavlova
leap, the final hug and kiss,
claws into flanks, jaws
in the spinal cord, and
the gazelle is fresh meat only.
Tableau: to the right
a blurring of dust, survival

of the fittest; in the foreground
the queen of beasts, prima donna, panting
hugely.
She buries her head
in the warm belly; blood
illuminates the grass. Sweetbreads
and tripe, the best parts first,
then the shredding
of muscle from bone: the thighs,
the pectorals—finally
sculpture, the graceful
leg bones unveiled, rib cage
exhibited.
Casually, like a tabby
turning away from a bowl, the queen
lumbers to the flickering banyan shade,
makes herself comfortable as a sphinx,
head on paws, and sleeps. The scene
gathers pace, no longer a two-
character drama. Seedy extras,
waiting in the wings,
pick up their cues: hyenas,
drooling through all that gormandizing,
clown their way to center
and rake off strips of flesh;
vultures drop out of the sky
like tent flaps in a gale,
upstaging the barking hyenas,
and beak into bones: the skeleton
goes bare, instant fossil. Evening
whimpers across the veldt; in minutes
dark drops in, the vultures exit;
little creeping things come out
and nibble at leftovers, mousy
silhouettes, getting
in each other's way, Marx
brothers in a panic; and
the immortal cockroach,

under a kleig-light moon,
shuffles through her late
late show.

2
This is how it's done: at Tierra del Fuego
we stalk the coast, naked as Spirits—we
are the great hunters, rocks
and slings ready for blood. When
the Spirits are kind to us, floating
a dead whale into shore, we hack at it
with sharp stones, delicious
rancid blubber, feasting
till our bellies bulge; make
ponchos out of the blubber,
holes for our heads, and nibble
the edges slowly, our deepest bones
feeling the twilight of
no lucky whales, no seals.
On easy days, we send the women
to dive for sea-eggs, or bait
the small fish in the bay; we streak
our faces white with clay
to please the Spirits: these
are the good times.
But the sins of wicked people,
wasters of food,
bring the screaming winds; then
the hungry nights come on.
We lie in ambush: if
we can trap the evil
tribesmen to the sunrise,
the feeding on their soft parts
will be sacred; but
if we cannot, there are still
the old women.
They feel it coming:
when babies are squalling for milk

and young breasts have gone dry
and bellies are snarling like curs,
they know it's coming,
the old women:
their eyes go big in their heads—
will it be me, the first,
or her? And when? How
long will you bear this hunger?
Sometimes
the eyes go wormy with waiting,
and at night they run away, but
we always find them in the hills
and drag them back to our fires.
At last
we have starved long enough.
We take the oldest first, a strong man
on each arm, each leg; we hold her face
over the fire, the head
jerking in smoke, her screaming
and twisting so weird, kids
mimic the squeals. Soon
she is food, enough
for our little clan: we cut her
carefully, keeping the best
for the hunters, strength
to defy the snows. Boys
get the next best pieces, then
the women and girls.
Old women come last: fingers
and toes, enough to hold them
till it's their turn. We
suck the broken bones
and burn them in our fires, Tierra
del Fuego; by the time the sun
betrays us to the dark,
everyone in the world
is happy.
The cucarachas come out

and taste the bloody earth,
twitching their whiskers. We chew
a few roaches, crunchy and tart,
and snuggle together, back to belly
for the long night, remembering
that somewhere in shadows
the Spirits watch: all-powerful, and
to be feared.

    3

This is how it's done: after the head-on,
drivers and passengers totalled;
after the flashing lights
bloody the neighborhood; after the sirens
yammer in, spewing stretchers;
after the tow truck jams carcasses
into the curb; after that,
it's her turn:
while vermin a hundred
million years old
swarm in the walls of air-
conditioned apartments,
she pulls up behind the Impala and begins.
First the whitewalls—hubcaps, wheels,
bolt by bolt, into the back
of her van: already
it's a good night's work,
and she's just begun.
Crowbar the trunk: the spare,
a suitcase, tool kit—gravy.
Then inside: blankets, jacket,
the C.B. A Cougar pulls over;
she bares her teeth: Listen,
this baby is mine,
you want business, take the Rabbit.
Now the front end: under
the sprung-open hood,
the socket wrenches:

alternator, battery, maybe
the carburetor . . . Well,
that's enough. The little guys
are getting pushy; leave them something,
hyenas, savages, they go
for scraps—tail lights,
wipers, spark plugs—all that comes later,
then the dousing of gas,
and the campfire without marshmallows.

That is how it's done: now
it is night;
fires are burning carrion bones
and the tawny leather of Jaguars.
It is not dark
or quiet; but it is night,
and everywhere the immortal
cockroach is busy
surviving.

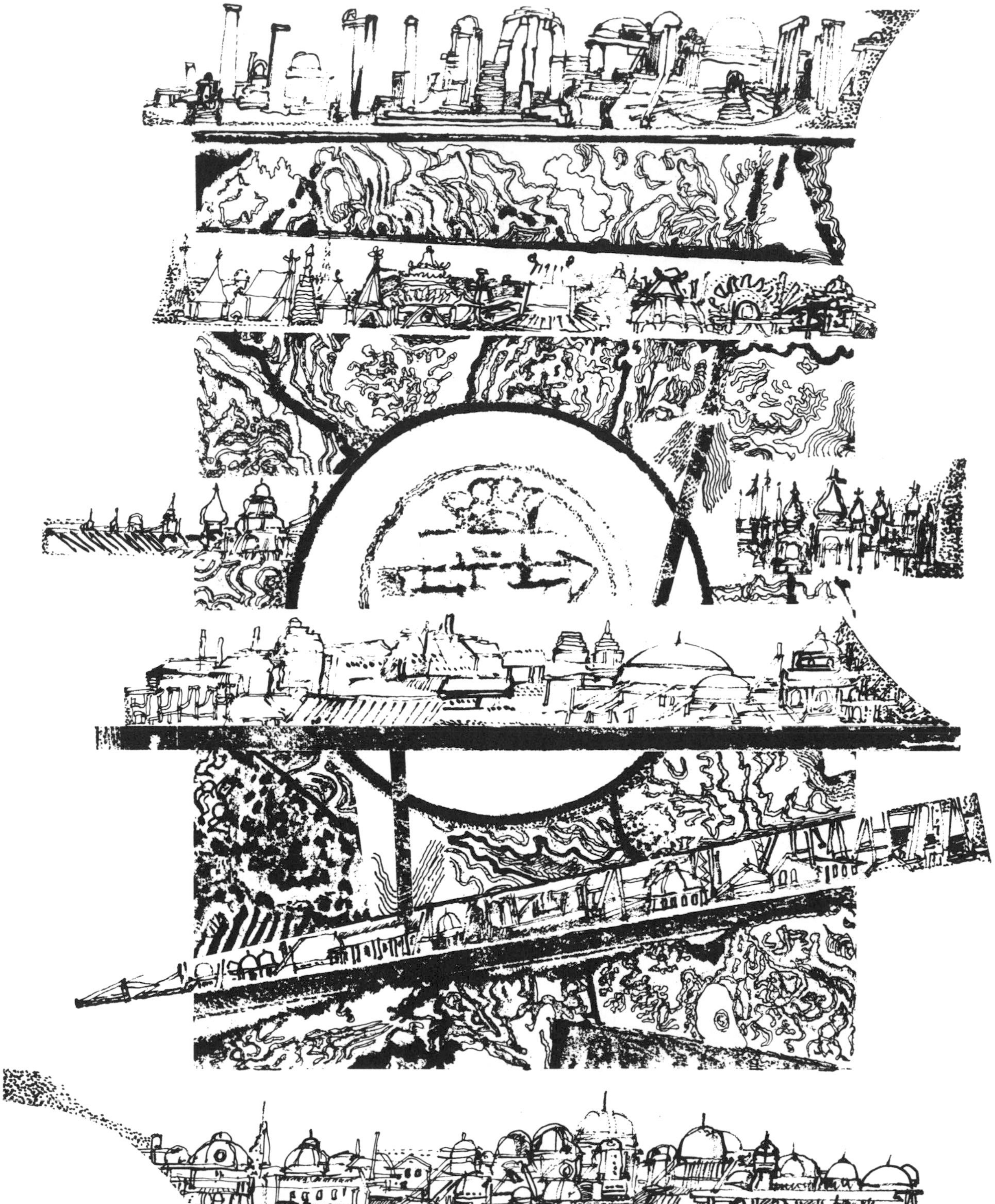

II

The Rust of Civilizations

Picture to yourself the chance
of your wife and your little children
being torn from you and sold
like beasts to the first bidder.
And these deeds are done by men
who profess to love their neighbours as
themselves, who believe in God,
and pray that His Will be done on earth.
It makes one's blood boil, yet heart tremble,
to think that we Englishmen
and our American descendants,
with their boastful cry of liberty,
have been and are so guilty.

CHARLES DARWIN

"Faith" is a fine invention
When gentlemen can see—
But microscopes are prudent
In an emergency.

EMILY DICKINSON

The Hand-Ax

Many things are at hand . . . wars, famines,
plagues, earthquakes . . . (but) let not your mind
be in any way disturbed; for these (are but) signs
of the end of the world . . .
>   Pope Gregory the Great
>   to King Ethelbert of England, 601 A.D.

To those who fully admit the immortality of the
human soul, the destruction of our world will not
appear so dreadful.
>   CHARLES DARWIN,
>   Autobiography, 1876

Under the topsoil, shards,
brick, the rust
of civilizations: we're young enough
to wonder at those relics, the sharks,
the horseshoe crabs, but old enough to know
the wreck of prophecy,
the fall of shamans, death
of temples—so
beyond the Book, beyond the Word,
beyond the Byzantines and Romans,
we dream of something older,
something walking upright, carrying
in the strong hand
this: one side round
for the palm, the cutting edge
fierce as a snarl, survivor
of a million years of sabre-tooth
and woolly mammoth, survivor of
those decadent flint arrowheads, bronze spears.
Hefting it now, here in the snow,
testing the ragged edge at Eighth Street
and Broadway, I know calluses, blood,
in the winter wind the smell
of red meat.
I pull on furs
and say goodbye to the fire in the cave,
to my woman and child,

to the old ones warming their skinny hands,
and step into bluster, scanning the smooth
snow till the tracks begin, doe and fawn,
bark fresh-nibbled. My moccasins
glide on the crust, the ax in my right hand
a constant urge; rabbits
skitter away, I sniff the air for tigers.
Two days' forest to the rising sun
my father's brother's clan
will join us for the bison kill
when the sun is making the long days;
but here there is only my own:
my spirits, my pines
green in the snow,
my animals.

They are upwind, chewing on saplings; I glide
across snow, nearly on them
before they turn—the quick alarm,
the scramble, awkward four-legged rush,
the doe gone like a spirit, but
the fawn is mine: the hand-ax
in one ecstatic blow
crushes the skull. I thong
her legs to a low limb,
slit the velvet throat, and drink,
warm to my moccasins.
Over my shoulders, the fawn's weight
breaks the crusted snow. Two days' forest
to the setting sun
my brother's woman's clan will come
to my naked cave in the long nights
to paint the deer and bison on the walls,
blood-red and ochre, soot-black—we have
the art now, in our cunning fingers,
learned from my father's cousin's shamans,
five days' forest to the standing star, magic
so the beasts will not escape us ever:
we shall feed, and feed again, our spells
so powerful that the ax,

in the holy blessing of blood and fire,
will some day find a handle, a blade,
find caissons and wheels, and roll
across the land, working deadly
miracles.

Pulling at the zipper on my coat,
I slog through snow,
holding my ancient stone at Eighth Street
and Broadway. I know, if I drive the glaze
two hours to sunrise, I will find
the stones of Jericho and Babylon
and two hours to sunset
the brick of Bethlehem:
in all this wasted land
no lions now to lie down with the lambs.
The magic of the hand-ax stripped the forests,
plowed the grasslands, led us
to the mushroom skies, the boiling clouds—so now
the hardest of all revolutions:
spray-painting walls blood-red and ochre,
soot-black, defiance to the hunger of the ax,
knowing our hands must join
to put a force to No,
to Never:
after a million years of axes, we
are old enough to know
that when we die
we die forever,
and so, to join hands
to break the ax of Tribe, the power
of shamans to wreck our lives
and kill forever
with the radiation-death
of a hundred thousand years—
strong enough to say to all of them:
we are *Homo sapiens*, smart animal;
we will not flame to passion
in the firestorms of your frenzy.

Darwin on Fourteenth Street

Vision at this depth
is blurred—in the muddy gutters
manta rays switch their poison tails;
above them cruise
the shadowy tiger sharks—this
is Fourteenth Street:
a hundred thousand diatoms
in the belly of a shrimp,
two hundred shrimp
in the belly of a herring,
five hundred herring
in the belly of a whale: this
is Fourteenth Street.

In Andalucía

"Very dry. Since three years,
little rain." Simple Spanish
so we'd understand. "The crops
are weak." His eyes tightened, the squint
of a grudging land.
We had come for the paintings, the animals
that fed Cro-Magnon here;
but for now, in the shade, we talked.
"A bad time," someone ventured,
needing to apologize for
the sparkling coast, our tall hotels.
"*Sí. Muy malo.*" A silence
as long as a sigh: the gray mountains
went on being mountains; in the distance
a truck was grinding its slow way up
and up—Andalucía, poorest province
of a poor country.
Sun shredded through
the cane shelter, the sweat of our climb
cooled, we thought of the long drive back,
twisting down to the coast;
we were ready for caves.
He gave us lanterns: splendid,
the gloomy halls, the chasms,
frozen cascades, the massive pillars
and icicles of stone, all
with their touristy names, Tower
of Pisa, Sword of Damocles, Bath
of the Moorish Queen. Then suddenly
all pretending stopped:
the limestone walls were human,
the hunter with his deadly bow
and his deathless prey, the graceful
running horse, the deer,
the long-horned mountain goat, the big fish
with little fish in its belly—

twenty thousand years
of eating. The cool
of the cave filtered
through our bones.
Emerging into glare,
we rubbed our arms like January,
making conversation:
"Do you guide in winter, too?"
"Yes. But very few
tourists in winter."
Muy poco, *muy seco*, *muy malo*, the stingy
history of this land: his eyes
did the painful squint again.
We started down.
The mountainsides were relentlessly
beautiful, corn and melons
fought the sun for life, peasants hoed
at the dusty earth: twenty
thousand years.

"Black-Footed Ferret Endangered"

The taste in our mouths
is the feeding of tigers:
we're killing off eagles, too,
and whales.
How it all began: the way
our thumbs slowly came round
to grab for the throat, our toes
flattened for stalking, more than animal
cunning
swelling the skull—and then
the clever tools: the hand-ax,
the motor, more dangerous
than tigers.
It was only a matter of time
till the tools were a part of us
like glands, a million years of murder
creating this:
the pitiless face of the tiger
is our own face grinning
with gears.

Reading Our Times

The social instincts . . . must have been acquired
by man in a very rude state, and probably even
by his early ape-like progenitors.
        DARWIN, *The Descent of Man*

This is the land of silk
and honey: a million baths of wine,
a hundred million measures of wheat,
pearls and onyx, alabaster,
tribute from far countries . . .

Straphangers in green fatigue
sling their rifles, the Bronx
quivers in the rumble of our Times:
    BIOLOGICAL WARFARE STUDIED, SPECIES
    ENDANGERED, CHURCH
    MILITANT, DEATH PENALTY
    REIMPOSED.
We finger our .45's
for practice, and another child
is bombed by practicing
Christians in Belfast,
and the bombing goes on somewhere
in the Holy Land, and the neutron bomb
is cannonized for National
Honor—
we shift our prehensile grip
and brace ourselves, rumbling
along with our Times,
south to the tropical fevers:
    SENATOR SEES STRUGGLE FOR EXISTENCE,
    SPECIES ENDANGERED,
    PRIMATES DENOUNCE THE TIMES.

. . . pearls and onyx, alabaster,
tribute from far countries, purple sails
from Tyre and Tarshish bearing
ivory, apes, and peacocks . . .

Jungle roots
are clutching at our tunnel, Grant's Tomb,
Columbia, Tropic of Cancer, Lincoln
Center, the heat is getting
unbearable, a hairy arm
shifts a cartridge belt; we slip
the catch off Safety and begin again, our Times
screaming through torrid zones, Columbus
Circle, Penn Station—pages go limp,
we feel for the trigger
and it happens: the penalty
reimposed, brakes
hissing like gas chambers, we stop
dead
between stations,
tunnel walls seeping
jungle rain, the monsoons up there
raking the banyans;
hang on, a guerrilla is screaming, remember
your Honor,
the good of the species,
the pride of the corps: so we hang on,
hang on, veins pumping baboon blood,
pores breathing gibbon brine, reading
our Times:

    EVANGELIST CALLS FOR GREAT CRUSADE,
    BOMBS KEEP PEACE, SAYS GENERAL,
    SPECIES ENDANGERED.

. . . purple sails
from Tyre and Tarshish bearing
ivory, apes, and peacocks —this
is the promised land, the land
of promises.

We sit here in the stillness of our Times
and it is only a brief delay, there is nothing
as long as our Times,
and soon we're rumbling again, due south,

Franklin, Chambers: the penalty
reimposed, we read on,
knowing that what we are reading
is the long report of our death,
time and place,
probable cause, survivors—and at last
we push through the bars
to Wall Street, promised land,
land of silk and honey, bearing our Times
into the screaming of monkeys,
into the streaming baobab,
ivory, apes, and peacocks,
hacking at dripping lianas
with our machetes, tracking the gamy spoor
of Honor.

After the Faith-Healings

The laying-on of hands: faith
that could move these barren hills
pulses through our fingertips,
and Darwin's demon apes of hell
howl the name of blasphemy.
We cast them out—yea, and the Serpent
who deceiveth the world, that
whoredom sitting on the waters,
with whom the kings of earth
have committed fornication, our faith
will cast it out! For so it was
by that little creek in Tennessee,
three hundred of the faithful come
marching to Zion in the August sun,
to pray above our crippled brother
seven raptured hours, and sing
   All hail the power of Jesus' name
till every hill in Tennessee
believed; and sisters in the throng, adrift
in all that heat and joy, were fainting for love
of the Lord, and men with muscles like the rocks
in God's good earth
watered the weeds with tears;
and when at last our hands came down
and touched those withered legs,
the afflicted brother stared around
with eyes that rolled with the love
of Jesus—and slowly rose, *rose,*
till he was on his knees,
our hymns still ringing off the hills:
   My faith looks up to Thee —
and then, in the heavenly current
coursing through our fingers, that
chosen man
set his teeth and rose again—
rose upright, in a tide of holy pain,

to stand on his own feet—stood there
a minute by the clock, before he slid
to grass! Praises, then, our praises rang
across the state of Tennessee—
for the Lord healeth those that are broken, He
telleth the number of the stars
and calleth them by their names—oh, Lord,
ravish our hearts with love
in the perfume of Thine ointments, in honey
and milk, in the savor
of saffron and pomegranates, come
to us now, Lord, come
as You did that sunny day in Tennessee—
come to us now as You came
to the halt and lame, to the woman
blind with cataracts, five hours in prayer, all
the faithful on that hilltop
shouting love to heaven, till
the demon shrieked aloud
and she was Saved, staring
into the sun till her dead eyes found
visions, omens crawling in the sky
that no one else in all that throng could see.

For so it has been, too,
here in the City of Angels, Zion of the West,
home of our Tabernacle, borne
from Tennessee, to fight
the poison plagues of Darwin on
the shores of this great ocean—here too
we have touched the fevered and palsied, here
we have said to the blind and bent:
"Thy faith hath made thee whole."
This boy, now,
fair and virginal, undefiled by woman, yet
possessed by the demon called
in the Godless clinic, "diabetes"—
this child was Saved,

as clear as Jesus' Word, washed
in the blood of the Lamb, as ready
for heaven as earth—the boy
had prayed with us, and his father
prayed, until their faith grew strong; and
here in these browning hills, we gathered
the faithful in our hundreds, chanting
till sunset:
    Praise God from Whom all blessings flow —
and the father, in that hour of triumph,
tears of good tidings on his cheeks,
called above the chanting,
"Come out of the boy, thou unclean spirit!"
And at that cry of victory,
he threw away the pills, those ugly
relics of his doubt—
and the boy cried out, rejoicing!

But oh, ye children of the light:
what terrors after sunset, in the hours
when Satan stalks the heathen dark
wherein the beasts of the forest move,
when Darwin's monkeys squeal their dirty lust,
and lions roaring after their prey do seek
the meat of God. The boy
had schooled with infidels, his faith
was thin like his youth, not robust
like his father's manly Grace—after two nights
the child would not breathe as he should,
his tongue went thick, perverse. Seven
of the faithful stayed always
and chanted at his bed till dawn, and he waxed
stronger for a moment here, a minute there—
then wavered, waned, refused to sing the hymns.
"Father," he whispered,
in a voice that spoke the spells of midnight,
"Father, give me the pills"—we heard the Serpent
slithering among us: the smell

of evil filled the room. Air! Light! We rushed
the boy in blankets to the hills
and faced him to the rising sun, and chanted,
    Nearer, my God, to Thee . . .
"Give me the pills," he whispered. But
his father's faith held strong; he cradled
the small head in his arms and sang,
    Holy, holy, holy, Lord God Almighty!
    Early in the morning our songs shall rise to Thee!

By the third verse, morning smog
had shut off the sun,
and in the swirling mist the demon rose,
Darwin's great beast rose before us,
scarlet with abominations—Satan
passed his hand over the boy's
sick faith: cold
settled in his limbs.

Oh, Lord,
Thou art Alpha and Omega, beginning and end,
and what is man, that Thou art mindful of him?

But yet he is not dead—the boy
only sleeps in the Lord. Tomorrow
he will rise again, our strength
will quicken his, the father's
sainthood will cast out this demon, Death,
and the boy will wake: here, on this
same hill, here in the sun in the City of Angels,
a thousand of the faithful sing from dawn
to sunset, praising the bountiful Lord,
and tomorrow we shall command this child to rise
and glorify God on earth, his body whole and strong,
his faith healed by the laying-on of hands,
the abiding prayer: tomorrow, yes,
tomorrow he will rise.

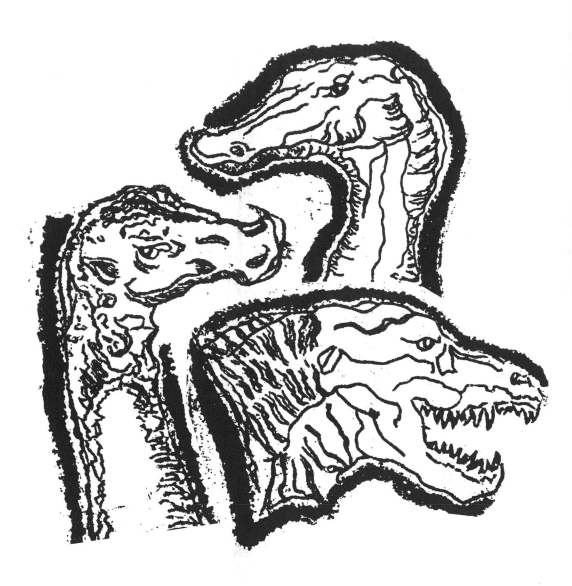

III

Animals Tame and Animals Feral

Young crocodiles
snap their little jaws
as soon as they emerge from the egg.

*

Lizards, when cooked, yield a white meat
which is liked by those whose stomachs
soar above all prejudices.

*

A taste for collecting beetles
is some indication
of future success in life.

                    CHARLES DARWIN

One wants to keep one's hand in, you know,
in every type of poem, serious and frivolous
and proper and improper.

                    T. S. ELIOT

DARWIN'S BESTIARY

Prologue

Animals tame and animals feral
prowled the Dark Ages in search of a moral:
the canine was Loyal, the lion was Virile,
rabbits were Potent and gryphons were Sterile.
Sloth, Envy, Gluttony, Pride—every peril
was fleshed into something phantasmic and rural,
while Courage, Devotion, Thrift—every bright laurel
crowned a creature in some mythological mural.

Scientists think there is something immoral
in singular brutes having meat that is plural:
beasts are mere beasts, just as flowers are floral.
Yet between the lines there's an implicit demurral;
the habit stays with us, albeit it's puerile:
when Darwin saw squirrels, he saw more than Squirrel.

1. The Ant

The ant, Darwin reminded us,
defies all simple-mindedness:
Take nothing (says the ant) on faith,
and never trust a simple truth.
The PR men of bestiaries
eulogized for centuries
this busy little paragon,
nature's proletarian—
but look here, Darwin said: some ants
make slaves of smaller ants, and end
exploiting in their peonages
the sweating brows of their tiny drudges.
Thus the ant speaks out of both
sides of its mealy little mouth:
its example is extolled
to the workers of the world,
but its habits also preach
the virtues of the idle rich.

2. The Worm

Eyeless in Gaza, earless in Britain,
lower than a rattlesnake's belly-button,
deaf as a judge and dumb as an audit:
nobody gave the worm much credit
till Darwin looked a little closer
at this spaghetti-torsoed loser.
Look, he said, a worm can feel
and taste and touch and learn and smell;
and ounce for ounce, they're tough as wrestlers,
and love can turn them into hustlers,
and as to work, their labors are mythic,
small devotees of the Protestant Ethic:
they'll go anywhere, to mountains or grassland,
south to the rain forests, north to Iceland,
fifty thousand to every acre
guzzling earth like a drunk on liquor,
churning the soil and making it fertile,
earning the thanks of every mortal:
proud *Homo sapiens*, with legs and arms—
his whole existence depends on worms.
So, History, no longer let
the worm's be an ignoble lot
unwept, unhonored, and unsung.
Moral: even a worm can turn.

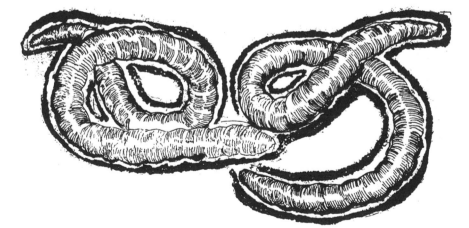

3. *The Rabbit*

a. Except in distress, the rabbit is silent,
   but social as teacups: no hare is an island.
      (Moral:
      silence is golden—or anyway harmless;
      rabbits may run, but never for Congress.)

b. When a rabbit gets miffed, he bounds in an orbit,
   kicking and scratching like—well, like a rabbit.
      (Moral:
      to thine own self be true—or as true as you can;
      a wolf in sheep's clothing fleeces his skin.)

c. He populates prairies and mountains and moors,
   but in Sweden the rabbit can't live out of doors.
      (Moral:
      to know your own strength, take a tug at your
         shackles;
      to understand purity, ponder your freckles.)

d. Survival developed these small furry tutors;
   the morals of rabbits outnumber their litters.
      (Conclusion:
      you needn't be brainy, benign, or bizarre
      to be thought a great prophet. Endure. Just endure.)

4. The Booby and the Noddy

They live on St. Paul's Rocks, the booby and the noddy,
the former is a gannet and the latter is a tern.
They're dumber than their looks, the booby and the noddy,
and there's a moral in it, as sure as you were born.
They go about their tricks, the booby and the noddy,
living for the minute with a featherheaded scorn
for intruders; Darwin coaxed the booby and the noddy
and knocked them in the bonnet at high noon; and Darwin learned
that they were so relaxed, the booby and the noddy,
that survival on this planet seemed none of their concern.
But soon they learned the facts, the booby and the noddy:
when you see a British pundit, it's time that you were gone;
and now they sing this text, the booby and the noddy:
mad dogs and Englishmen go out in the noonday sun.

5. The Dog

Keep your eyes on his tail: upright and stiff,
look out—he'll go from bluff to rough
before you can cough. On the other hand,
you know the mutt is man's best friend
when his tail's between his legs. We all
had tails once—the belle
of every ball, every duke
in embryo, every thug,
every cardinal and bishop.
And frankly, it seems to be a tossup
whether we're better off without.
Our pants are easier to fit,
it's true—but think of what we've lost.
How many times have all of us guessed
wrong about a person? Think
how different, if, instead of a blank
look, or mute expression of guile,
we all had an honest tail to tell.

6. The Gossamer

Sixty miles from land the gentle trades
that silk the Yankee clippers to Cathay
sift a million gossamers, like tides
of fluff above the menace of the sea.

These tiny spiders spin their bits of webbing
and ride the air as schooners ride the ocean;
the *Beagle* trapped a thousand in its rigging,
small aeronauts on some elusive mission.

The Megatherium, done to extinction
by its own bigness, makes a counterpoint
to gossamers, who breath us this small lesson:
for survival, it's the little things that count.

Mr. Extinction, Meet Ms. Survival

They're always whispering:
missing buttons, crow's-feet,
rust—
and I try to ignore them at first,
but they keep it up:
half-soles, dry rot,
biopsies, Studebakers—
that does it,
and I have to yell back:
virgin wool! fresh coffee! tennis balls!
new pennies! robins!
and that holds them awhile,
but they always come again,
sometimes at night, sometimes
in crowded elevators: *loose shingles,*
they whine, *soil erosion, migraines,*
dented fenders. I hold my ears
and shout: *high tide! fresh bread!*
new shoes! oranges! and people around me nod
and straighten their shoulders and smile,
and I think for a moment I've won—
but of course you never win,
and it gets to be almost a game:
they give me *oil spills,*
sewage sludge, tobacco smoke;
I come back with *swimming pools,*
butterflies, corn fields!
They give me *Calcutta,*
Gary, Coney Island;
I rattle off *Windermere,*
Isfahan, Bloomington! But
by the time I'm at work
'it gets serious, all
lapsed memberships and *auto graveyards*
and *partial dentures* and *sub-*
committees and *leaves in the eaves,*

and right there at my desk I bellow:
daffodils! and *sailboats!* and *Burgundy!*
and *limestone!* and *birch trees!* and *robins,*
damn it, robins! and my boss
pats me on the shoulder, and my secretary
takes it in shorthand, and everywhere
efficiency doubles, I'm doing it, after all,
for them. And yet,
deep down, I know, in fact,
it's no more daffodils than it's half-soles—
what it really is,
is morning without a hangover
but an even chance of rain,
it's a cost-of-living raise
and a slight case of heartburn; well,
we all know about
the slow leak, the scratch
on our favorite record,
the 7:12 forty minutes late, sure—
but passenger pigeons? Studebakers? That's
going too far,
we have our pride, our good
intentions, our metabolism, we won't
be shunted off with clipper ships
and whooping cranes, we're going
to hang in there, all of us, because
the robins may be showing wear,
but still, by god,
they are robins.

Darwin's Ark

Queasy again, and feeling
as wintry as Methuselah,
Darwin begins to drowse, and thinks,
as he always does, of animals, all
those animals, and remembers
his leafy days at Cambridge, chasing beetles
and cramming for the Ministry: the Testament
in Greek, the classy proofs
of God's design—and in that jungle
of memories, he drifts off, and dreams
that he is Noah, seed of Methuselah, already
six hundred years old, more than a little tired
from all that virtuous living—and then (just
his luck) a finger out of the clouds
pokes down at him, and a voice
like a celestial sergeant commands:
"Make thee an ark of gopher wood. . ."
The details follow, in that same
platoon-leader's voice: the boat shall be
four hundred fifty feet long,
seventy-five feet wide, three decks,
one window, one door.

    And then
    the voice tells him why.

His sons, Shem, Ham, and Japheth, just
cannot handle this news:
"He's going to drown them *all*?" Japheth whispers,
"Every last woman and child? But why?"
Noah's mind isn't what it used to be; lately
it strays like a lost lamb: "Uh—
wickedness, I believe
that's what He said—yes, wickedness."
Too vague for Japheth: "But wicked *how?* I mean,
what are the charges, exactly?"
The old brow wrinkles again: "Evil, that's

what He said. Corruption. Violence."
"*Violence?* What do you call
this killer flood—this pogrom—this Final
Solution of His? He's going to deep-six
the lot of them, just
for making a few mistakes? For being—*human*?"
Now Japheth was really riled; being the youngest,
he still had a lot of drinking buddies out there—
Enos and Jared, and raunchy Adah
and his pretty young neighbor,
Zillah—together they'd put away
many a goatskin of red wine
under the big desert stars. Besides,
being a kid, a mere ninety years old,
he still enjoyed stumping his father
with embarrassing questions: "Listen,
Dad, I thought you said He
was omniscient—well, then,
wouldn't He have foreseen all this? And if He did,
then why did He make us the way we are,
in the first place? Just think of all this
useless trouble, the waste,
the genocide!"

"Ours not to reason why," says Shem (the first-born,
and something of a prig), "Ours but to build the ark."
"And that's another thing," Japheth scowls,
"what *is* an ark, exactly? I mean,
we're desert people, right?—nomads,
living out here in this miserable dry scrub
with our smelly goats and camels—
I never saw a boat in my life."
"Well, I saw one once," Noah quavers,
"but I don't remember it very well,
that was four hundred years ago—
or was it five, let's see. . ."
"Concentrate, Dad," says Ham,
always the practical one, "Look,

it can't be that hard, an ordinary boat,
we'll mock one up, no problem—a keel,
that's it, you begin with a keel of gopher wood,
and the rest is easy: ribs, then planks,
pitch, decking—listen,
just give me a crew of hard-hats, say a hundred
of those wretched condemned sinners out there,
and I'll handle it."

So finally they had themselves an ark,
and God says, "OK, Noah,
get the animals—clean beasts, seven of a kind,
unclean, just two, but make sure
they're male and female, you got that straight?
Now hurry it up, I'm itching to get
the drowning started."
Noah had thought that this
would be the easy part, but Japheth,
of course, knows better: "Dad,
did you say *every* animal?"
"Every animal," Noah repeats,
quoting Authority: " 'Every living thing
of all flesh'—fowl,
cattle, creeping things, the works.
Plus food enough for a year."

Well, just imagine: you're living out there
in that abominable desert, and all of a sudden
you're supposed to come up with two elephants.
Or is it more? "Shem—Shem, is the elephant
a clean or an unclean animal—
if it's clean, that means seven of them,
and the ark is in trouble. And how
about rhinos? hippos? And what do we do
about the dinosaurs? How do we get a brontosaurus
up the gangplank?" Japheth, of course,
loved raising problems that Noah
hadn't thought of at all: "Pandas—kids

love pandas, we can't let them drown,
but how do we get two of them here
in a hurry, all the way from China?
And, oh, by the way, Dad,
how are we going to keep the lions
away from the lambs?''

Let's face it, it was a nightmare:
the apes and monkeys were bad enough—
gibbons, orangutans, gorillas, chimps,
howler monkeys, spider monkeys, squirrel monkeys,
capuchins, mandrills, baboons, marmosets—
just think of poor Ham, after all of his angst
and sweat, getting the ark assembled, and then
having to schlepp off to the Congo, the Amazon,
to bring 'em back alive, all those tricky
long-tailed leapers, up in the jungle greenery.

And Shem, dutiful Shem, in charge
of the other mammals—the giraffes,
the horses, zebras, quaggas, tapirs, bison,
the pumas, bears, racoons, weasels,
skunks, mink, badgers, otters, hyenas,
the rats, mice, squirrels, gophers, beavers,
porcupines, rabbits, hares, bats,
sloths, anteaters, moles, shrews—thousands
of species of mammals.

And Japheth out there on the cliffs and treetops
trying to snare the birds: the eagles,
condors, hawks, buzzards, vultures, and every
winged beauty in the Field Guides, and bring them back,
chattering, twittering, fluttering around
on the top deck—thousands on thousands
of hyperkinetic birds.

   Two by two
   they come strolling through:

antelope, buffalo, camel, dog,
egret, ferret, gopher, frog,
quail and bunny, sheep and goose,
turtle, nuthatch, ostrich, moose,
ibex, jackal, kiwi, lark,
two by two they board the ark.

Well, it's pretty clear, isn't it,
that we've got a space problem here: a boat
only four hundred fifty feet long, already buzzing
and bleating and squeaking and mooing
and grunting and mewing and hissing and cooing
and trumpeting and growling and roaring and snarling
and chirping and peeping and clucking and croaking—
and the crocodiles aren't back from the Nile
yet, or the iguanas from the islands,
or the kangaroos and koalas, or
the pythons or boas or cotton-mouth moccasins
or the thirty different species of rattlesnake
or the tortoises, salamanders, centipedes, toads . . .

It took some doing, all that,
but Ham came back with them,
and wouldn't you know,
it's Japheth who opens up, so to speak,
the can of worms: "Worms, Dad! There are thirty-two
thousand species of worms—who's
going digging for *them?* And oh, yes—
how about the insects?"
"Insects!" Shem, old Goody-Two-Shoes, rebels
at last. "Dad, do we have to save *insects?*" Noah,
faithful servant, quotes the Word:
"every living thing." "But Dad, the cockroaches?"
Noah has all the best instincts
of a minor bureaucrat: he
is only following orders; the roaches
go aboard.

But it turns out, the insects almost
break up the team, because
this is not just anybody's dream,
this is Darwin's dream, so of course
Japheth knows too much. "Look, Dad,
we've got dragonflies, damselflies, locusts, and aphids,
grasshoppers, mantises, crickets, and termites . . .
Wait a minute—termites?
You're going to save termites—in a wooden boat?"
But Japheth knows that arguing with Noah
is like driving a nail into chicken soup—he shrugs
and ticks away at his clipboard:
"We've got lice, beetles, God knows
(pardon the expression) how many beetles;
we've got bedbugs, cooties, gnats, and midges,
horseflies, sawflies, bottleflies, fireflies,
we've got ants, bees, wasps, hornets—
can you imagine what it's going to be like
locked in with *them* for a whole year?
But listen, Dad, we haven't scratched the surface—
there are nine hundred thousand species
of insects out there, did you happen to know that
when you took this job?
Even if we unload all the other animals,
the insects alone will sink the ark!"

Ah, but the ark was not floating on fact,
it was floating on faith: that is to say,
on fiction—and in fiction, the insects
went aboard, all nine hundred thousand
buzzing, stinging, chittering, biting species,
and a year's supply
of hay for the elephants, a year's bananas
for the monkeys—"OK," Japheth says,
"But you still haven't answered my question—
what will the meat-eaters eat?"
"We'll cross that bridge when we come to it,"

Noah replies, in history's
least appropriate trope. "Come on,
all aboard; it's starting
to sprinkle."

The east wind, full of broth,
bullies the bay windows, and Darwin
stirs in his sleep, losing the ark
for a moment, seeing Brazil again,
the rain forests, the insects, blue-
green, vermilion, saffron—all
those beautiful insects . . .

Well, the fountains of the great deep
were broken up, and the windows of heaven opened,
and the rain was upon the earth
forty days and forty nights,
and the ark was lifted up
and went upon the face of the waters,
and the floundering began outside, the running
for the hills. Noah knew it was happening,
and so did Shem and Ham, snug
as a bug on A deck; but
it was hard-boiled Japheth who howled and keened
for Enos and Jared, still out there
somewhere, and Adah and beautiful Zillah,
so he was the first to break and run
for the one small window; and yes,
there it was, just the way fear
had been painting it on his eyelids ever since
that divine command: the fighting
for high ground, crazed beasts goring
and gnashing, serpents dangling from trees.
Then Shem and Ham and finally Noah
and the four nameless wives
couldn't resist; they ran for the window
and watched their friends and neighbors
hugging in love and panic until

they all went under. Japheth caught
one final glimpse, and of course it had to be Zillah,
holding her baby over her head
till the water rolled over her
and she sank, and the baby
sank, splashing a little, and then
there was silence upon the waters,
and God was well pleased.
They all turned away from the window, Noah
and his boys, and their weeping wives,
and no one in the ark would look
at anyone else for many days.

So, for a solid year that strange menagerie
lived in the ark, the sixteen thousand hungry birds
lusting for the eighteen hundred thousand insects,
and the twelve thousand snakes and lizards
nipping at the seven thousand mammals,
and everyone slipping and sliding around
on the sixty-four thousand worms
and the one hundred thousand spiders—
and Noah driving everyone buggy, repeating
every morning, as if he'd just thought of it:
"Well, we're all in the same boat."

   (Oh, in case you're wondering, Noah
   conveniently
   forgot about the dinosaurs:
   even in miracles, enough
   is enough.)

It was a long, long year. Imagine,
if you will, the trouble
for those washed-out men and their bedraggled wives,
feeding the gerbils and hamsters, cleaning
the thousands of cages, keeping the jaguars
away from the gazelles, the grizzlies away
from the cottontails—everything aboard, after all,

was an endangered species.
And imagine those seven clean elk,
clashing antlers at mating time,
and imagine Noah, with his brittle bones, trying
to dodge all those rattlers and copperheads
and vipers and cobras and scorpions and
black widows and tarantulas; and imagine—oh, imagine
cleaning up after the elephants
for a whole year, swabbing those
unspeakable decks . . .

    But enough—
    our sleeper is stirring.

Darwin starts out of his bad dream, sweating,
and lies there thinking of Noah.
Darwin knows all about death, and extinction, and so
he understands
the sinking heart of poor old Noah,
after the waters subsided,
and the dove fluttered off and never returned,
and the gangplank slid to Ararat,
and the animals scampered out to the muddy,
corpse-ridden earth—Noah,
burning a lamb on his altar

under that relentless rainbow, remembering
that he rescued the spiders and roaches, but
he let Enoch and Jubal
and Cainan and Lamech and
their wives and innocent children
go to a soggy grave—and Darwin knows
that Noah knows, in his tired bones,
that now he will have to be fruitful once more,
and multiply, and replenish the earth
with a pure new race of people who
would never, never sin again,
for if they did,
all that killing would be
for nothing, a terrible
embarrassment to God. And Noah knows
that just like his grandpa, Methuselah,
he will be obliged to live
with his strangling memories
for another three hundred years.

PHOBIAS

Fear is the most depressing of all the emotions.
CHARLES DARWIN, *The Expression
of the Emotions in Man and Animals*

1. Gaminophobia: the fear of ten-year-olds

The imagination of something dreadful commonly
excites a shudder.   IBID.

Small shadows in your doorway:
last week they were playing hopscotch
when Mrs. Green came home;
she will never identify them.
Sometimes you see them
through your darkened blinds, little elves
breaking into stores: you think
of phoning the cops; you do not get involved.
They play games with the locks of your building,
sharding their half-pints in stairwells;
you wish them luck, dreading the time
they run short. So far you have always
made it home with the groceries, but
you know there will come a time
when the little ones will need you.

2. Mortiphobia, the fear of self-reproach

Under a keen sense of shame there is a
strong desire for concealment.

I am the bony arm
around your throat, the clutching
deep in your guts.
When your heart flips like a bad TV,
it's me.
I know just how much you can take:

I give you a little more.
Don't scream; that music
excites me.
At noon you may get away,
but I'll have you again at sundown.
If you thought last night was bad,
wait till three A.M.: I have something
special in mind, involving
clammy sheets, and moaning
in your sleep.
I'll be waiting.

3. Shamanophobia, the fear of specialists

Prostration follows, and the mental powers fail.

One way or another, they get you:
if not on options or futures,
then lab tests and diagnostics,
the x-ray gun at your head.
Since childhood you've dreaded their sine curves,
alpha particles, parameters; for years
you've suffered from prosody,
econometrics, phenomenology.
But now you swear you are turning
a new leaf: you will make an in-depth study
of semiotics, commodities, Mendelian ratios,
endothermic reactions, hermeneutics . . .
You are wrong: you will never know
the right word for anything; you will not know
the runic languages, the cuneiform;
you will not know
the Chinese ideogram for death.
You will lie in an unmarked grave.

4. *Locophobia, the fear of crazies*

We feel horror if we see any one exposed to danger.

Harmless, everyone says, but you know
they're not. He comes at you on the bus,
yelling a language you don't understand.
You keep your eyes on the *Times;* he lurches on,
clutches a girl in the back; she screams.
You want to say Hey, cut that out,
but you're no fool, you read the *Times.*
The screaming girl is fed up:
she belts him with her bag;
he goes down, gets up; she hits him again.
The bus pulls into a stop;
he staggers to the door, and out, yelling
something you don't understand.
Everyone smiles: yes, that one
was harmless. You read the *Times* closely.
You wait for the next one.

5. *Bacardophobia, the fear of neighborhood liquor stores*

There is a sudden and uncontrollable tendency to headlong flight.

In your community
it is always rum, small bottles snuggling the hip.
Sometimes they are able to pay, but
if they need your help
they will ask for it; in your community
false modesty is not a major
social problem.
In good times, in your community
it is a nonstop block party,
the empties smashing in gutters.
In bad times, you see them coming for you;
you wish you could cross the street,
but over there, others of your community
are waiting.

6. *Phobiophobia, the fear of fear*

The word "terror" ought to be confined to cases in which
the imagination is more particularly concerned.

All you have to fear
is fear itself, all you need hate
is hate; love, love; isn't it swell
that it's all so simple?
Never again will you shrink
at the dark in a doorway, the smoke
in your midnight bedroom, an outer door
slightly ajar. You will go
willingly on unscheduled flights,
disregard ladders and cats,
feel easy on observation decks,
in elevators, empty rooms.
No: all you have to fear now
is the thing creeping up behind you
wearing your face.

EUPHORIAS

1. *Waldorf-Astoria Euphoria, the joy of big cities*

Joy, when intense, leads to various purposeless movements—
to dancing about, clapping the hands, stamping, etc.   IBID

You feel so good, you stop walking:
they swirl around you, racing the 6:15.
You bless them all with a smile
you cannot explain: they are suddenly
precious. You look around, with your alien eyes,
at forty floors of windows where
they are laughing, talking, and kissing: you realize
they are priceless. You feel them
under the pavement, riding the uptown express,
straphanging bodies waving
like kelp, and you know
they are irreplaceable; you think of them
all over town, bursting
with unused happiness, and you clap,
and clap again, and clapping, you sing
a song you thought you'd forgotten, and your waist
moves gently, like jonquils, and your hand
catches her fingertips, and she smiles, her arms
moving like willows,
and the fruitseller dances with apples,
crying a musical language, and a girl
with a bongo comes on with rhythm,
her hips moving like wheatfields, and
the hardhats come up from the manholes,
their bodies moving like jackhammers,
and Chinese voices like windchimes
sing to the women from San Juan

who gather around like palm trees, and the cops
have cordoned the street and are dancing
with women from Minnesota,
their thighs as seductive as seaweed;
and you know that sooner or later
this had to happen: that somehow
it would all break out, all that pent-up
joy, and people would sing and hold hands,
their bodies swerving like taxis,
and the music inside their heads
would fill the streets with dancing,
clapping hands, and stamping;
and you sing another chorus
of we,
hey, we,
yes, we,
I said we
are all
we've got.

2. Peoria Euphoria: the joy of small towns

A man smiles . . . at meeting an old friend in the street.

You find yourself drifting
on decades: the elms are immortal, arching
the red brick street. At Main
the concrete is veined with tar,
bubbling in sun. You test it
with bare toes: hot,
exciting, all the skin
you've never touched, telling you
of houses unlocked,
cars with keys inside, faces of women
as open as summertime—Jean,
after all these years, still dying
in the senior class play,
Sally, dissecting her ancient frog,

Mary, who still believes
in Jonah's whale. They smile at you,
and you smile, of course, you can't help it,
you are all so delighted that nothing
ever changes.

3. *Hunkydoria Euphoria, the joy of having it made*

> From the excitement of pleasure, the circulation becomes more
> rapid, the eyes are bright, and the colour of the face rises.

You're sweating it out: the last time
it was never received;
it was lost in the files; sent
to the wrong department.
If you get there by noon, surely
it will be all right; but the seconds
are deadly. At ten to twelve
you reach the office, and of course
there's a line.
You inch along; at noon you touch
mahogany, and just as you feared, there is
some difficulty, a shuffling
of papers: you feel
the invisible stars
swing through their long
cold journey. Finally—
you can hardly believe it—
it's there! the very thing! the thing itself!
and the holy rubber stamp
falls like a benediction,
and you hear, above the ceiling,
the seraphim rejoicing,
and you smooth your hair
and borrow a debonair manner
and step through the frosted door
so deliberately,
no one would ever guess
that right there under your shirt
the sun is dancing on water.

How Evolution Came to Indiana

In Indianapolis they drive
five hundred miles and end up
where they started: survival
of the fittest. In the swamps
of Auburn and Elkhart,
the jungles of South Bend,
one-cylinder chain-driven runabouts fall
to air-cooled V-4's, 2-speed gearboxes,
16-horse flat-twin midships engines—
carcasses left behind
by monobloc motors, electric starters,
3-speed gears, six cylinders, 2-chain drive,
overhead cams, supercharged
to 88 miles an hour in second gear, the age
of Leviathan . . .
There is grandeur in this view of life,
as endless forms
most beautiful and wonderful
are being evolved.
And then
the drying up, the panic,
the monsters dying: Elcar, Cord,
Auburn, Duesenberg, Stutz—somewhere
out there, the chassis of Studebakers,
Marmons, Lafayettes, Bendixes, all
rusting in high-octane smog,
ashes to ashes, they
end up where they started.

So Full of a Number of Things

I fell asleep on the grass, and awoke with a chorus of
birds singing around me, and squirrels running up
the trees . . . and it was as pleasant and rural a scene
as I ever saw, and I did not care one penny how any
of the beasts or birds had been formed.

Darwin to his wife, Emma, 1858

It is better than crabs in curry,
better than icy beer
or tangerines, this
feeling, this
sudden, crazy feeling that
is better than Brahms on stereo,
better than harem girls on velvet or
beach boys in cocoa butter,
better than *Hamlet*, better than Mr.
Universe, this
sudden and perfectly sensible feeling
that is better than carpeted bathrooms
or double-breasted suits,
better than finding a quarter
or seeing a kangaroo or
holding a smooth
stone—this feeling,
here in the afternoon sun,
that our grimy street is opening up
to one long windy beach,
and every pigeon on the block
is already a soaring gull,
and we're standing out here on the sand,
and we suddenly feel sure,
without any doubt at all,
better than Plato or Revelation,
that tomorrow the taste of sunrise
will be better than crabs in curry,
better than icy beer
or tangerines.

I V

In the Caves of Childhood

Man, with all his noble qualities,
with sympathy which feels
for the most debased,
with benevolence which extends
not only to other men but
to the humblest living creature,
with his god-like intellect which
has penetrated into the movements
and constitution of the solar system—
with all these exalted powers—
man still bears in his bodily frame
the indelible stamp
of his lowly origin.

CHARLES DARWIN

I do not belong to the class of literary people
who take a skeptical attitude toward science;
and to the class of those who rush into anything
with only their own imagination to go upon, I
should not like to belong.

ANTON CHEKHOV

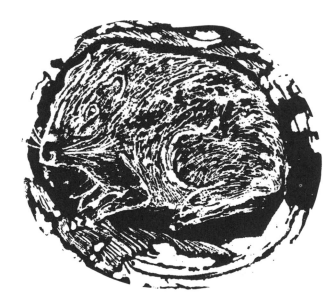

How My Light Is Spent

Eyes are certainly not necessary to animals
having subterranean habits.
      DARWIN, *The Origin of Species*

On the subway you thought
it couldn't happen to you. But now
the doctors are dazzling in white, Science
burns in your eyeball: white-equals-black.
At last
the true dark falls like an eyelid.
In the waiting room, your hand reaches out
for a white cane: the dark
is an old home, you live there
in the caves of childhood,
with your lovers in lamplight,
with the brown hair of your beautiful sisters.
In the down elevator you think:
but everybody sees. What you see
in the shine of the car is Science,
dazzling in white, Darwin
dissecting his blind
barnacles; you see moles, bats,
fins in the murk
of a thousand fathoms; now
you know better. At the door
daylight staggers you; hands over face,
you find the subway. There,
in dim fluorescence: the Byzantine
mosaic of the walls,
I-beams rich with perfect rivets,
the silver splendor of the rails,
and from a green bench, as the gorgeous
graffiti scream in,
a woman in a crimson sweater
rising like the sun.

Staying Awake with Darwin

One whole night I tried to think over the pleasure
of seeing Shrewsbury again.
                    Darwin at Valparaiso

In the throb of the all-night bus
at its terminal stop, in the lonely click of heels
in concrete canyons are
moonshadows of maple leaves
on Indiana sidewalks, sleepless birds
sending their liquid keening into
a honeysuckle midnight:
the popcorn wagon with golden wheels,
lemon cokes at the Palace of Sweets,
DeSotos and Terraplanes
bearing eager arms to some
quick privacy, caverns of bulls
and bison, a glimmer
in the mind's eye, till
back in the real world, a cast of thousands
thunders across the morning, carrying off
the mockingbirds—but tonight
it will happen again, and tomorrow night,
the faces in your darkened streets gone
young as unwritten books, innocent
of yesterday: mothers, fathers, hunters,
painters of caves
will be staring down the future,
and in their childlike eyes will be
shifting dunes and windswept beaches, nothing
anywhere to build on.

The Descent of Man

House knocked down
to the highest bidder,
V-8 back on the lot,
clothes to charity, mail
returned "Unknown":
then
the walk into the trees, dropping
shoes, pants,
underwear—and cross-legged
in the clearing, the slit-eyed
concentration: now to know only
the back of the hand, bristles riding
the easy articulation, the swinging
from branch to branch—
and the claws, jutting and keen,
going straight for the eyes of killers.

Sexual Selection

Accounting for
his balding majesty, Tiberius,
squirming to fellatio by a suckling babe,
and
the meanest pimp on Forty-Second Street;
accounting for scandalous temples in India
and
silken seraglios in Stamboul;
accounting for the wrath of Achilles, the wreck
of Sampson, Antony, Edward the Eighth
and
small-town studs with greasy hair
is
the stimulus of terminal neurons in the genitals
transmitted to subcortical areas of the brain
by an autonomic network of synapses
which
return the standard sensations
to the groin.

"Sea Otter Survival Assured"

We saw several sea otters, the fur of which is held
in such high estimation.
DARWIN, *The Voyage of the Beagle*

The Fish and Game Department reports 591 otters in
the current census, 94 higher than last year.
NEWS REPORT

A million years before Darwin
this weasel slid into the sea
to tear at the brooding oysters
and roll wet eyes for the gliding
shadows of dim sea-monsters.
For a million years of birth
in the brine of the north Pacific
the fair exchange was fur
like ermine. When the big boats came,
bearing the hairless hunters,
the fittest betrayed his survival:
his skin was worth more than his life.

In a fog, five hundred otters
are nudging their young along
the coastline of California,
while monstrous in bed, the Pacific
is breaking with billions of faces,
turbaned men from the Punjab,
brown-eyed girls with rice bowls,
horsemen waving their rifles—
and five hundred otters thrashing
the bell of a bedside alarm.

Survival assured: across
the pacific waves of blanket
someone as blond as hope
speaks from the edges of sleeping:
"Morning is out there again,
on the other side of the curtains."

Natural Selection,
we have come through another night,
come to one more day.

On the *Beagle*

Some people hold the world
in their fingertips, and
are part of what they hold.

The *Beagle* set sail
to easy summer—five years on sea
and land the watchful man
from Cambridge put
his fingers on a universe
of cuttlefish, sea-slugs, condors,
the ancient monsters' bones,
Megatherium, Mastodon: all
fixed forever in immutable forms, creatures
of a benign Intelligence.
It was written.

But the young man put his fingers on
the pulse of rivers, coral reefs,
pampas and mountains,
the flotsam of earthquakes—and
on futures of learning, from
pigeons' plumage, the beaks of finches, bones
of rabbits and ducks—decades
of learning,
dissecting ten thousand
barnacles—pondering:
"If we choose to let
conjecture run wild, then animals—
our fellow brethren in pain,
disease, death, suffering, and famine—
they may partake from our origin
in one common ancestor:
we may be all
netted together."

The *Beagle* labored on: in the winter
of Cape Horn,

twenty-three days of beating
against the icy bluster
came to broken boats
and spoiled collections.
The good ship rode to shelter—
and there on a rocky point
of Tierra del Fuego, naked
in snow, a mother
suckled her child
("whilst the sleet fell and thawed
on her naked bosom, and on the skin
of her naked baby")—there, in a little band,
stood
"man in his primitive wildness,"
ringed by the dark beech forest:
"As they threw their arms wildly
around their heads,
their long hair streaming,
they seemed the troubled spirits
of another world."
There
in the Bay of Good Success,
Charles Darwin, on the foredeck of the *Beagle*,
our future in his freezing fingertips,
stared into the faces
of our past.

The Voyage Home

The social instincts . . . naturally lead to the golden rule.
DARWIN, *The Descent of Man*

1

Holding her steady, into the pitch and roll,
in raw midwestern hands ten thousand tons
of winter wheat for the fall of Rome,
still swallowing the hunger of the war:
the binnacle glows like an open fire,
east-southeast and steady,
Anderssen, the Viking mate,
belaboring me for contraband,
my little book of Einstein, that
"Commie Jew." (So much for the social instincts,
pacifism, humanism, the frail
and noble causes.) I speak my piece
for western civ: light bends . . .
stars warp . . . mass converts . . .
"Pipe dreams," says the Dane, "pipe dreams."
"Well, mate, remember,
those Jewish dreams made nightmares
out of Hiroshima, and
blew us out of uniform, alive."
He stomps down off the bridge; some day
he'll fire me off his rusty
liberty: I read too much.
The ocean tugs and wrestles with
ten thousand deadweight tons
of charity, trembling on
degrees and minutes. Anderssen
steams back in with coffee, to
contest the stars with Einstein, full ahead.
We haven't come to Darwin.

2

Freezing on the flying bridge,

staring at the night for nothing,
running lights of freighters lost
in a blur of blowing snow,
we hold on through the midnight watch,
waiting out the bells.
With Einstein in our wake, the tricks
are easier: liberty
churns on, ten knots an hour,
toward Rome. One starry night
we ride at last with Darwin on
the *Beagle:* endless ocean, sea
sickness, revelations
of Toxodon and Megalonyx—a voyage
old as the Eocene, the watery death
of Genesis. The going
gets rough again, the threat of all those bones
churning the heavy swells: Anderssen,
a true believer, skeptical,
and Darwin trapped in a savage earthquake,
the heave of coastal strata conjuring
the wreck of England, lofty houses gone,
government in chaos,
violence and pillage through the land,
and afterward,
fossils gleaming white along
the raw ridges.
"Limeys." Anderssen puts his benediction
to empire: "Stupid Limeys." After that
we breathe a bit and watch the stars and tell
sad stories of the death of tribes, the bones,
the countless bones: we talk about
the war, we talk about
extinction.

3

Okinawa, Iwo Jima:
slouching toward Tokyo, the only good Jap
is a dead Jap.
We must get the bomb, Einstein writes

to F.D.R., waking from
the dreams of peace, the noble causes:
get it first, before
the Nazis do. (The only good Nazi
is an extinct Nazi.)
At the death of Hiroshima, all day long
we celebrate extinction, chugalugging
free beer down at the PX, teen-
age kids in khaki puking pints
of three-point-two in honor
of the fire: no more island-hopping now
to the murderous heart of empire.
Later, in the luxury of peace,
the bad dreams come. "Certainly,"
Darwin broods, "no fact
in the long history of the world
is so startling as the wide and repeated
extermination
of its inhabitants."

4
Off somewhere to starboard, the Canaries,
Palma, Tenerife: sunrise
backlights the rugged peaks, as Darwin,
twenty-two years old, gazes at
the clouds along the foothills.
Longitudes ease westward; it's
my birthday: twenty-two years old
as Tenerife falls into the sunset,
I'm as greedy for the old world
as Darwin for the new, Bahia, Desire,
the palms and crimson flowers
of the Mediterranean, clear water
dancing with mines. Ahead of us
a tanker burns; the war
will never end.

5

"You talk a lot," says the melancholy Dane.
"You sure you're not Jewish yourself?
You got a funny name."
"Well, mate, I'm pure Celtic on one side,
pure Orphan on the other: therefore half
of anything at all—Jewish, Danish,
what you will: a problem, isn't it,
for Hitler, say, or the Klan,
or even Gregor Mendel, sweating out the summer
in his pea patch?"
The fact is, I know those ancestors
floating through my sleep:
an animal that breathed water,
had a great swimming tail,
an imperfect skull, undoubtedly
hermaphrodite . . . I slide
through all the oceans with these kin,
salt water pulsing in my veins,
and aeons follow me into the trees:
a hairy, tailed quadruped,
arboreal in its habits, scales
slipping off my flanks, the angle of my spine
thrust upward, brain
bulging the skull until
I ride the *Beagle*
down the eastern trades to earthquake,
to naked cannibals munching red meat
and Spanish grandees with seven names
crushing the fingers of slaves.
Who are my fathers? mothers? who
will I ever father?
I will sire the one in my rubber sea-boots, who
has sailed the seas and come
to the bones of Megatherium.
From the war of nature, from famine and death,
we stand at last creators
of ourselves: "The greatest

human satisfaction," Darwin muses, "is derived
from following the social instincts." Well,
the thing I want to father
is the rarest, most difficult thing
in any nature: I want to be,
knee-deep in these rivers of innocent blood,
a decent animal.

   6

Landfall: Yankee liberty discharges
calories on the docks, where kids
with fingers formed by hairy
quadrupeds cross
mumbo jumbo on their chests
and rub small signs for hope
and charity.
Liberty, sucked empty of its
social instincts, follows the *Beagle*
down the empty avenues of water
to amber waves of grain, to feed
the children of our fathers' wars,
new generations of orphans, lives
our quaint old-fashioned bombs
had not quite ended.

   7

Alone
on the fantail
I hear the grind of rigging, and
Darwin is beside me, leaning on the rail,
watching the wake go phosphorescent.
We've been out five years, have seen
the coral islands, the dark skins
of Tahiti; I have questions.
"Darwin," I whisper, "tell me now,
have you entered into the springs of the sea,
or have you walked in search of the depth?
Did you give the gorgeous wings to peacocks,
or feathers to the ostrich?

Have you given the horse his strength
and clothed his neck with thunder?
Who has put wisdom in the inward parts,
and given understanding to the heart?
Answer me."
The breeze is making eddies in the mist,
and out of those small whirlwinds come the words:
"I have walked along the bottom of the sea
wrenched into the clouds at Valparaiso;
I have seen the birth of islands and
the build of continents; I
know the rise and fall of mountain ranges,
I understand the wings of pigeons,
peacock feathers, finches; my mind creates
general laws out of large
collections of facts."
The rigging sighs a little: God
is slipping away without
saying goodbye, goodbye to Jewish dreams.
"But the activities of the mind,"
Darwin murmurs, "are one of the bases of conscience."
Astern the pious Spaniards go on praying
and crushing the fingers of slaves; somewhere
the Mylodon wanders away,
out of the animal kingdom and
into the empire of death.
For five billion years
we have seen the past, and
it works.

   8
So this is the final convoy
of the social instincts: the next
time missiles fly to Rome,
they will carry Einstein's dream of fire,
and afterward there will be no need
for liberties, hope, or charity.
Now we ride the oceans of
imagination, all horizon

and no port. Darwin
will soon be home, his five-year
voyage on this little brig
all over; but when will I
be home, when will I arrive
at that special creation: a decent animal?
The land is failing the horizons, and
we only know to take the wheel
and test the ancient strength of human struggle,
remembering that we ourselves, the wonder
and glory of the universe, bear
in our lordly bones the indelible stamp
of our lowly
origin.